"The Mysteries of The Bible"

Hidden Danger

Copyright © 2024 by Dr. Anthony Ladson

All rights reserved. No part of this book may be used or reproduced by any means, graphic, electronic, or mechanical, including photocopying, recording, taping, or by any information storage retrieval system, without the written permission of the publisher except in the case of brief quotations embodied in critical articles and reviews.

"How Yoga Poses Challenge Christian Faith Beyond Exercise"

Contents

Introduction 1

Overview 5

The Tree Pose 21

Warrior I, II, and III Poses 23

Half Moon Pose 25

The Splits Pose 27

The Standing Pose 29

The Goddess Pose 31

Shiva Is "The Lord of Yoga"! 33

My Appeal to You 35

What God Says About Practicing Yoga 45
    Scriptures Warning Against Worshiping Other Gods, Practicing Yoga, Offering Up to Idols, and Worshiping Demons 45

The Deception and Appeal to Believers 64

Hope for Deliverance 65
    Scripture for Encouragement: 67

Stories of Deliverance..71
Closing Thoughts 81
About The Author..83

Introduction

Yoga is widely celebrated as a path to physical health, mental clarity, and spiritual tranquility. However, beneath its serene surface lies a profound and potentially perilous spiritual dimension. In this book, "Hidden Dangers: How Yoga Poses Challenge Christian Faith Beyond Exercise" we delve into the deeper meanings of various yoga poses and their connections to Hindu deities. Many practitioners may not be consciously aware of this spiritual link, but it is inherent in the practice. By engaging in these physical exercises (asanas) and breathing techniques (pranayama), individuals can tap into the spiritual realm and potentially encounter supernatural influences.

Numerous yogic texts and yoga websites support this connection. For example, one source states, "As a way of connecting to, revering, and paying respect to deities, many yoga postures represent not just what the deity looks like, but also everything they stand for. As we practice the posture, we put our focus on the energy and essence of the deity and look to embody their qualities."

Pause and consider that carefully. When practitioners assume yoga poses dedicated to specific gods and goddesses, a spiritual association occurs, transferring the "energy and essence" of those deities into the practitioner. The goal is to embody these divine qualities. Essentially, yoga positions are acts of worship (pujas), through which the traits of the deities worshiped become part of the practitioner's heart and life.

If these deities truly existed as perfect, benevolent gods, such a connection might be seen as beneficial and healthy. However, what if they are merely mythical constructs, products of human imagination? If that is the case, what is the source of the 'transformational influence' claimed by proponents of this aspect of yoga practice? This is a question we will delve into further as we continue.

Traditionally, Hinduism is said to have 330 million deities (though some sources claim 33 million). This number likely serves as a poetic expression of the vast array of divine beings within the Hindu pantheon, rather than an exact count.

Hidden Danger

The spiritual dimensions of yoga are often hidden in plain sight, seamlessly woven into the fabric of poses and practices that seem purely physical. This subtle integration is part of what makes yoga so appealing and, simultaneously, so potentially dangerous. Practitioners might enter a yoga class seeking stress relief or physical fitness, unaware that they are participating in a form of worship. Somewhere in that class is some shape or form no matter how small it is, there is an altar to that specific deity. The serene environment, the calming music, and the gentle instructions all serve to mask the deeper spiritual significance of the asanas.

Consider the Tree Pose, which symbolizes stability and growth, and is associated with Lord Vishnu, the preserver of the universe. Or the Warrior Poses, which honor the fierce warrior Virabhadra, an incarnation of Lord Shiva. Each of these poses is not just an exercise but a form of veneration, a physical manifestation of spiritual principles.

This book aims to uncover these hidden connections, revealing how yoga, often seen as a benign practice, can be a gateway to spiritual realms and influences. We will explore the specific poses and their associated deities, examining the implications for those who practice yoga, particularly from a Christian perspective.

As a born-again believer, it is crucial to understand these hidden dangers. The Bible warns against worshiping other gods, practicing idolatry, and engaging in activities that can lead to spiritual compromise. This book will provide insights and guidance on how to navigate these complexities, offering a path to deliverance for those who seek it.

In the following chapters, we will delve deeper into each pose, exploring their origins, meanings, and spiritual implications. We will also discuss the overarching themes of yoga, including its ultimate goals and the potential risks for Christians. This journey will uncover truths that are often hidden in plain sight, challenging you to reconsider the spiritual impact of yoga and its place in your life.

Overview

Yoga's Hidden Spiritual Dimension: Yoga is more than a physical exercise; it is deeply entwined with spiritual practices and Hindu deities. This book, "The Hidden Dangers: How Yoga Poses Could Invite Worship to Hindu Deities," aims to uncover these hidden connections. By engaging in yoga poses (asanas) and breathing techniques (pranayama), practitioners might unknowingly tap into the spiritual realm and invite supernatural influences.

Unconscious Acts of Worship: Many yogic texts and websites affirm that yoga postures are ways to connect with, revere, and pay respect to deities. This means that when you practice these poses, you might be inviting the "energy and essence" of these deities into your life, aiming to embody their qualities. Essentially, yoga positions can be acts of worship (pujas) that integrate the traits of these deities into your heart and life.

Mythical Constructs or Spiritual Entities?: If these deities were benevolent and real, the connection might seem beneficial. However, what if they are mere myths or human constructs? The 'transformational influence' claimed by proponents of yoga needs scrutiny. What is the source of this influence? This book will delve into these questions, examining the spiritual risks involved.

Vast Pantheon of Hindu Deities: Hinduism traditionally speaks of 330 million deities, a poetic expression of the numerous divine beings in its pantheon. This highlights the extensive spiritual landscape that yoga practitioners might unknowingly engage with.

Hidden in Plain Sight: The spiritual dimensions of yoga are often seamlessly woven into its physical practices, making them easy to overlook. Many enter yoga for fitness or stress relief, unaware they might be participating in a form of worship. The serene environment and calming practices can mask the deeper spiritual significance of the poses.

Christian Perspective: As a born-again believer, understanding these hidden dangers is crucial. The Bible warns against worshiping other gods, practicing idolatry, and engaging in activities that comprise spiritual integrity. This book will guide you through these complexities, offering insights and paths to deliverance for those who seek it.

Chapter Insights: Each chapter will delve into specific poses, their origins, meanings, and spiritual implications. We will discuss the overarching themes of yoga, its ultimate goals, and the risks for Christians. This journey aims to reveal truths hidden in plain sight, challenging you to reconsider yoga's spiritual impact and its place in your life.

A Call to Awareness: This book is a call to awareness for born-again believers. Understand the seriousness of practicing yoga and unifying with these deities. Equip yourself with knowledge and discernment to navigate the spiritual intricacies of yoga, ensuring your faith and spiritual integrity remain uncompromised.

The 3 Ingredients of Deity Yoga and How It Is Hidden in Plain Sight

Devotion and Surrender

While deity yoga might appear to rely on complex mantras and mudras (gestures) for effectiveness, its most crucial element is devotion. This practice requires an individual to genuinely desire to love and adore the deity without ulterior motives. Initially, practitioners might view the deity as a mere portal to spiritual experiences, but true devotion transcends such superficial goals. The deity gradually becomes the focal point of one's thoughts, emotions, and actions, dominating the waking state and even influencing dreams and deep sleep.

Over time, practitioners start seeing the deity in others and even in their own reflections, perceiving life circumstances as expressions of the deity's grace. This process is designed to lead to a complete surrender of personal claims and the offering of everything to the deity in pure, unconditional love. For born-again believers, this can be particularly deceptive. The allure of spiritual growth and inner peace might mask the subtle infiltration of a different spiritual allegiance. Devotion and surrender in deity yoga are not just about respect or admiration but about a deep, transformative relationship where the practitioner's will is aligned with the deity's supposed will.

An example of this hidden danger is how yoga sessions often begin with an invocation or dedication to a deity, cloaked in seemingly harmless intentions. A born-again believer might join a yoga class for its health benefits, not realizing that the opening chants and poses are acts of worship to entities incompatible with their faith. The chants are calling that deity and invoking his attention to you. This silent, gradual process of devotion can slowly shift their spiritual focus from God to these deities, drawing them into a form of idolatry without their conscious consent.

Mantra

Mantras, especially bīja (seed) mantras, play a vital role in deity yoga. Each bīja mantra corresponds to a specific deity and, when invoked, acts like a key fitting into a lock, unlocking deeper spiritual experiences. The mantra is most effective when it is infused with life through prolonged practice or initiation from a teacher who has mastered it. With steady practice and unwavering devotion, the mantra reveals deeper aspects of the practice, leading the practitioner closer to the deity.

For Christians, the use of mantras can be particularly insidious. These mantras, often recited repeatedly during meditation or yoga sessions, are not mere words but powerful invocations designed to invite the presence and influence of specific deities. For example, the common chant "Om" is often explained as a universal sound or vibration, but it is also deeply connected to Hindu spirituality and the invocation of various gods.

A born-again believer might be encouraged to incorporate these chants for their calming effects, not realizing they are inviting spiritual influences that conflict with their faith. This practice can create a spiritual dissonance, slowly eroding their commitment to God. The mantra, once established as a regular part of their routine, subtly shifts their focus and spiritual allegiance, making it a hidden yet potent tool for inviting the deity into their life.

Discernment and Dispassion

Through sustained devotion and mantra practice, practitioners of deity yoga cultivate discernment and dispassion. This cultivation allows the fundamental vibration underlying all creation to emerge in their consciousness. As this awareness deepens, practitioners begin to perceive intricate patterns and pathways, creating new neural and hormonal connections. Inner visions of sacred geometry, such as yantras and mandalas, arise spontaneously, integrating knowledge and experiences into a cohesive, unified whole.

This phase is particularly dangerous for born-again believers because it fosters a sense of spiritual enlightenment and unity with the universe that can be mistaken for genuine spiritual growth. The vivid inner experiences and feelings of interconnectedness can be compelling, leading believers to assume they are achieving a higher spiritual state. However, these experiences are designed to deepen the practitioner's bond with the deity, subtly redirecting their spiritual focus.

An example of how this can trick Christians is through the integration of these practices in mainstream wellness and mindfulness programs. A believer might engage in such a program, drawn by the promise of mental clarity and emotional balance, only to find themselves immersed in practices that cultivate this deceptive discernment and dispassion. The program's apparent benefits mask the spiritual compromise it entails, leading the practitioner to a path that distances them from their faith and aligns them with the deities behind these practices.

By understanding these three ingredients of deity yoga—devotion and surrender, mantra, and discernment and dispassion—born-again believers can recognize the subtle yet profound ways in which yoga can draw them into unwitting worship of Hindu deities. This chapter serves as a warning to remain vigilant and discerning, keeping one's spiritual focus firmly on God and avoiding practices that could lead to spiritual compromise.

Five Action Steps to Fortify Born Again Believers Who Have Been Tricked into Practicing Yoga

Recognize and Renounce Any Involvement

First and foremost, acknowledge and renounce any involvement in yoga practices that are connected to Hindu deities. Understanding the spiritual implications and openly renouncing these practices are crucial steps in breaking any spiritual ties.

Scripture: "And the times of this ignorance God winked at; but now commandeth all men everywhere to repent" (Acts 17:30, NKJV).

Repent and Seek Forgiveness

Confess and repent for participating in activities that invited other spiritual influences into your life. Ask God for forgiveness and cleanse your heart and mind from any spiritual residue left by these practices.

Scripture: "If we confess our sins, He is faithful and just to forgive us our sins and to cleanse us from all unrighteousness" (1 John 1:9, NKJV).

Renew Your Mind with God's Word

Immerse yourself in the Word of God to renew your mind and fortify your spiritual defenses. Replace the teachings and philosophies of yoga with the truth found in Scripture.

Scripture: "And do not be conformed to this world, but be transformed by the renewing of your mind, that you may prove what is that good and acceptable and perfect will of God" (Romans 12:2, NKJV).

Engage in Godly Practices

Replace yoga with godly practices that strengthen your faith and bring you closer to God. Engage in regular prayer, Bible study, and worship. Seek out Christian-based physical activities that honor God.

Scripture: "Meditate on these things; give yourself entirely to them, that your progress may be evident to all" (1 Timothy 4:15, NKJV).

Seek Fellowship and Accountability

Surround yourself with a supportive Christian community that can provide accountability, encouragement, and guidance. Engage in fellowship with other believers who can help you stay strong in your faith and avoid spiritual pitfalls.

Scripture: "And let us consider one another in order to stir up love and good works, not forsaking the assembling of ourselves together, as is the manner of some, but exhorting one another, and so much the more as you see the Day approaching" (Hebrews 10:24-25, NKJV).

By following these action steps, born-again believers can fortify themselves against the spiritual dangers of yoga and reaffirm their commitment to God. Recognizing the hidden dangers, renouncing past practices, and immersing oneself in godly activities will strengthen their faith and safeguard their spiritual well-being

The Ultimate Goal of Yoga

The ultimate goal of yoga extends far beyond physical fitness. It aims at spiritual awakening and union with the divine. This section delves into the philosophical underpinnings of yoga, emphasizing its transformative potential and the journey towards self-realization. However, for born-again believers, this spiritual journey can lead to stark and perilous realities.

The Deeper Spiritual Aim

Yoga is designed to guide practitioners toward a state of union with a higher consciousness or divine presence. This is achieved through various practices that cultivate physical, mental, and spiritual alignment. The ultimate goal is to invoke and invite the deity associated with specific yoga practices to become one with the practitioner. This spiritual union is considered the pinnacle of yoga, where the individual's consciousness merges with the deity's essence, resulting in profound transformation.

For born-again believers, this spiritual pursuit poses significant risks. The Bible clearly warns against worshiping other gods and engaging in practices that invite spiritual influences contrary to the Christian faith. Yoga's subtle integration of these practices can easily deceive even devoted Christians, leading them into a spiritual trap.

Invoking and Inviting Deities

The practice of invoking and inviting deities is central to yoga's spiritual dimension. Through mantras, mudras, and meditation, practitioners consciously or unconsciously invite these deities into their lives. The stark reality is that these deities, or demons as referred to in the Christian faith, respond to such invitations.

Imagine the scenario: a born-again believer, unaware of the spiritual implications, participates in yoga. They might feel a sense of peace or spiritual fulfillment, mistaking it for God's presence. In reality, they have unknowingly called upon a deity. If questioned about their presence in a believer's life, these deities could easily retort, "Hey!? I was minding my business and they called me and invited me to be yoked with them. I didn't call them, so that's why they do as I say."

Devotion and Surrender

Devotion and surrender are critical components of achieving yoga's ultimate goal. Practitioners are encouraged to devote themselves entirely to the deity, surrendering personal ambitions and desires. This process involves focusing all thoughts, emotions, and actions on the deity, leading to a deep, transformative relationship. The deity becomes the central figure in the practitioner's life, ruling over their consciousness.

For Christians, this practice is particularly dangerous. The gradual shift from devotion to God to devotion to a deity can occur subtly and deceptively. Yoga sessions often begin with invocations that seem harmless but are acts of worship to these deities. Over time, this devotion can erode a believer's spiritual foundation, leading them away from their faith.

Mantras: Keys to Spiritual Doors

Mantras, especially bīja (seed) mantras, are powerful tools in yoga for invoking deities. These mantras act like keys, unlocking spiritual doors and inviting the deity's presence. Through repeated chanting and meditation, practitioners deepen their connection with the deity, gradually aligning their consciousness with the deity's essence.

For a born-again believer, the use of mantras can be highly deceptive. The calming effects of chanting might be mistaken for spiritual peace, masking the reality of inviting a spiritual entity into their life. This practice can create a spiritual conflict, drawing the believer away from God and towards the deity, ultimately compromising their faith.

Discernment and Dispassion

Through devotion and mantra practice, yoga practitioners develop discernment and dispassion. This heightened awareness allows them to perceive the fundamental vibrations of the universe, leading to a sense of unity with the divine. However, for Christians, this can be a dangerous illusion. The profound spiritual experiences and inner visions may feel like enlightenment but are designed to deepen the bond with the deity.

An example of this deception is found in mainstream wellness programs that incorporate yoga. A Christian might join such a program for its health benefits, unaware of the spiritual dimensions. Over time, the practices can lead to a sense of spiritual awakening, which is actually a deeper connection with the deity. This false sense of enlightenment can draw the believer further from their faith, leading them to spiritual compromise.

Conclusion

The ultimate goal of yoga is not merely physical fitness but spiritual union with deities. For born-again believers, this poses a significant threat. By engaging in yoga, they risk invoking and inviting spiritual entities that conflict with their faith. Understanding these dangers and remaining vigilant is crucial to maintaining spiritual integrity and avoiding the deceptive allure of yoga's spiritual promises.

The Tree Pose

The Tree Pose, or Vrikshasana, appears as a simple balancing act but delves deep into spiritual realms. Dedicated to Lord Vishnu, the preserver of the universe, this pose is said to root practitioners into the divine strength and stability of Vishnu. As Christians, one must ponder the gravity of aligning oneself with a deity who stands in opposition to the One True God. The Bible warns against the worship of false gods, and Vrikshasana subtly entwines the soul with Hindu spirituality. The physical act of grounding oneself in this pose may symbolically root one's spirit into a foreign spiritual soil, drawing strength and balance not from Christ, but from Vishnu. Consider the eternal consequences: what strength does one truly gain when it comes from a false god? Embrace this practice, and you might find your spiritual stability shifting away from the cornerstone of Christian faith, leading to a subtle yet profound spiritual drift.

Summary of Key Points and Warning Signs

The Tree Pose

The Tree Pose, often viewed as a simple balancing exercise, is dedicated to Lord Vishnu, a deity representing stability and growth. Engaging in this pose symbolizes seeking spiritual alignment with this deity.

For born-again believers, this poses a risk of inadvertently inviting the deity's influence into their lives.

- Warning Sign: Performing poses dedicated to deities invites spiritual influences contrary to Christian beliefs.

- Scripture Warning: "You shall have no other gods before Me" (Exodus 20:3, NKJV).

Warrior I, II, and III Poses

Virabhadrasana, or the Warrior Poses, invoke the fierce spirit of Virabhadra, an incarnation of Lord Shiva. Each stance—Warrior I, II, and III—channels attributes of courage, strength, and focus, embodying the warrior's relentless spirit. However, for a Christian, this is not mere physical exercise but a spiritual act of channeling Shiva's warrior avatar. Shiva, the destroyer, represents a force diametrically opposed to the Christian God. As you strike these poses, consider the spiritual warrior spirit you are inviting into your life. The Bible speaks clearly against aligning with spiritual forces outside of God's dominion. Practicing these poses may subtly shift your spiritual allegiance, inviting the destructive and chaotic energies of Shiva into your soul. Reflect deeply: in your pursuit of physical strength and focus, are you sacrificing your spiritual purity and dedication to Christ?

Summary of Key Points and Warning Signs

Warrior I-II-III Poses

These poses, representing Virabhadra, a fierce warrior deity, embody strength and power. Practicing these poses can lead to spiritual identification with Virabhadra.

- Warning Sign: Aligning oneself with a warrior deity contradicts the Christian ethos of peace and reliance on God for strength.

- Scripture Warning: "For the weapons of our warfare are not carnal but mighty in God for pulling down strongholds" (2 Corinthians 10:4, NKJV).

Half Moon Pose

Ardha Chandrasana, the Half Moon Pose, is a graceful asana that pays homage to Chandra, the moon god. This pose invites calmness and balance, mirroring the tranquil light of the moon. Yet, for Christians, this seemingly benign practice may lead to spiritual disquiet. Chandra represents cycles, change, and reflection—qualities that, when spiritually aligned with, can shift one's focus from the steadfastness found in Christ. The Bible warns against aligning with celestial entities, as these practices can lead to idolatry. By practicing the Half Moon Pose, you are symbolically opening your soul to the influence of Chandra, risking the peace and serenity found only in Jesus. Consider this deeply: is the pursuit of balance worth the peril of spiritual misalignment? Embrace this pose, and you may find your spiritual life waxing and waning, just like the moon, unstable and reflective of a light not your own.

Summary of Key Points and Warning Signs

Half Moon Pose

Dedicated to Chandra, the moon god, this pose symbolizes balance and serenity. Practicing this pose can subtly invite the spiritual influence of Chandra.

- Warning Sign: Seeking serenity through poses dedicated to deities rather than through God's peace.

- Scripture Warning: "Peace I leave with you, My peace I give to you; not as the world gives do I give to you. Let not your heart be troubled, neither let it be afraid" (John 14:27, NKJV).

The Splits Pose

Hanumanasana, or the Splits Pose, honors Lord Hanuman, the monkey god revered for his devotion and strength. This pose symbolizes dedication and the power to overcome obstacles through faith and determination. For Christians, however, this dedication should be solely towards God. Hanuman's mythology, rich with tales of divine monkey strength, stands in stark contrast to the worship and reverence due to Jesus Christ. By embodying this pose, you are not just stretching your body but potentially stretching your spiritual allegiance. The Bible cautions against idol worship and the veneration of other gods. Consider the spiritual ramifications: in seeking physical flexibility and strength, are you bending your devotion away from God? Reflect on this deeply—embracing Hanumanasana could lead to a spiritual split, a division of loyalty between Christ and a false god.

Summary of Key Points and Warning Signs

The Splits Pose

Associated with Hanuman, a monkey god, this pose signifies devotion and service. Practicing this pose can symbolize a spiritual connection with Hanuman.

- Warning Sign: Engaging in devotional poses to deities invites non-Christian spiritual influences.

- Scripture Warning: "You shall not make for yourselves a carved image—any likeness of anything that is in heaven above, or that is in the earth beneath, or that is in the water under the earth" (Exodus 20:4, NKJV).

The Standing Pose

Tadasana, or the Mountain Pose, is the bedrock of many yoga practices, grounding practitioners to the earth with a sense of rootedness. This pose is associated with Prithvi, the earth goddess, invoking stability and a deep connection to the earth. Christians should be wary, as this grounding is not just physical but spiritual. The Bible emphasizes worshiping God alone, and grounding oneself spiritually in Prithvi's energy can lead to subtle idolatry. By practicing Tadasana, you might find yourself spiritually rooted in the earth's energy rather than the solid rock of Christ. Reflect on the consequences: is the feeling of physical stability worth the risk of spiritual disorientation? By embracing this pose, you may inadvertently shift your spiritual foundation away from God, leading to an erosion of your faith and devotion.

Summary of Key Points and Warning Signs

The Standing Pose

This pose, representing Tadasana, symbolizes a mountain and stability. It's dedicated to the strength and endurance of deities.

- Warning Sign: Seeking stability and strength through poses dedicated to deities instead of relying on God.

- Scripture Warning: "The Lord is my rock and my fortress and my deliverer; my God, my strength, in whom I will trust" (Psalm 18:2, NKJV).

The Goddess Pose

Utkata Konasana, or the Goddess Pose, is a powerful stance that venerates divine feminine energies. Associated with goddesses like Durga and Kali, this pose embodies strength, protection, and transformation. For Christians, invoking these deities through practice is spiritually perilous. Durga and Kali, while symbolizing strength, also represent forces and principles that stand outside the Christian faith. The Bible warns against the worship of other gods, and practicing the Goddess Pose might invite these powerful, yet spiritually foreign, energies into your life. Consider the gravity of this act: in seeking empowerment and transformation, are you invoking forces that could spiritually mislead you? Reflect deeply on the implications—embracing this pose could transform not just your body but your spiritual allegiance, leading you away from the true power and protection found in Christ alone.

Summary of Key Points and Warning Signs

The Goddess Pose

Dedicated to various female deities, this pose symbolizes feminine power and fertility. Practicing this pose can invite the essence of these deities.

- Warning Sign: Invoking feminine deities contradicts the Christian understanding of God's power and creation.

- Scripture Warning: "For there is one God and one Mediator between God and men, the Man Christ Jesus" (1 Timothy 2:5, NKJV).

Shiva Is "The Lord of Yoga"!

Lord Shiva, revered as the Lord of Yoga, is a central figure in many yogic traditions. His influence permeates through numerous poses and practices, guiding practitioners towards a union of consciousness and bliss. For Christians, this poses a significant spiritual conflict. Shiva, as the god of destruction and transformation, embodies principles that are fundamentally different from Christian teachings. The Bible strictly admonishes the worship of false gods, and aligning with Shiva through yoga can lead to a dangerous spiritual syncretism. As you delve into yoga practices under Shiva's influence, consider the ultimate consequence: are you pursuing enlightenment at the cost of your soul's devotion to Christ? Reflect on this deeply—embracing Shiva as the Lord of Yoga might lead you into spiritual practices that estrange you from the true path of salvation found only in Jesus.

Summary of Key Points and Warning Signs

Shiva is "The Lord of Yoga"

This chapter highlights Shiva's central role in yoga as the destroyer and transformer. Engaging in yoga practices can subtly align a believer with Shiva's influence.

- Warning Sign: Associating with a deity whose attributes conflict with Christian teachings.

- **Scripture Warning: "Therefore put to death your members which are on the earth: fornication, uncleanness, passion, evil desire, and covetousness, which is idolatry"** (Colossians 3:5, NKJV)

Conclusion

The ultimate goal of yoga is not merely physical fitness but spiritual union with deities. For born-again believers, this poses a significant threat. By engaging in yoga, they risk invoking and inviting spiritual entities that conflict with their faith. Understanding these dangers and remaining vigilant is crucial to maintaining spiritual integrity and avoiding the deceptive allure of yoga's spiritual promises.

My Appeal to You

In this final chapter, we reflect on the spiritual dimensions of yoga and its impact on practitioners' lives. As a born-again believer, it is crucial to recognize that yoga practices should not be part of your spiritual journey. The allure of physical benefits can mask deeper spiritual risks. The ultimate goal of yoga extends far beyond physical fitness. It aims at spiritual awakening and union with the divine. This chapter delves into the philosophical underpinnings of yoga, emphasizing its transformative potential and the journey towards self-realization. However, for born-again believers, this spiritual journey can lead to stark and perilous realities.

If you find yourself entangled in these practices, know that deliverance is possible if you choose to seek it. This chapter summarizes the key points discussed in previous chapters, highlighting the warning signs and emphasizing the need for mindfulness and awareness of yoga's deeper spiritual implications.

Summary of Key Points and Warning Signs

The Ultimate Goal of Yoga

Yoga aims at spiritual awakening and union with deities, which can lead to born-again believers inadvertently inviting these entities into their lives.

- Warning Sign: The ultimate goal of yoga conflicts with the Christian pursuit of union with God alone.

- Scripture Warning: "And what agreement has the temple of God with idols? For you are the temple of the living God. As God has said: 'I will dwell in them and walk among them. I will be their God, and they shall be My people'" (2 Corinthians 6:16, NKJV).

The Tree Pose

The Tree Pose, often viewed as a simple balancing exercise, is dedicated to Vrksasana, a deity representing stability and growth. Engaging in this pose symbolizes seeking spiritual alignment with this deity. For born-again believers, this poses a risk of inadvertently inviting the deity's influence into their lives.

- Warning Sign: Performing poses dedicated to deities invites spiritual influences contrary to Christian beliefs.

- Scripture Warning: "You shall have no other gods before Me" (Exodus 20:3, NKJV).

Warrior I-II-III Poses

These poses, representing Virabhadra, a fierce warrior deity, embody strength and power. Practicing these poses can lead to spiritual identification with Virabhadra.

- **Warning Sign**: Aligning oneself with a warrior deity contradicts the Christian ethos of peace and reliance on God for strength.

- **Scripture Warning**: "For the weapons of our warfare are not carnal but mighty in God for pulling down strongholds" (2 Corinthians 10:4, NKJV).

Half Moon Pose

Dedicated to Chandra, the moon god, this pose symbolizes balance and serenity. Practicing this pose can subtly invite the spiritual influence of Chandra.

- Warning Sign: Seeking serenity through poses dedicated to deities rather than through God's peace.

- Scripture Warning: "Peace I leave with you, My peace I give to you; not as the world gives do I give to you. Let not your heart be troubled, neither let it be afraid" (John 14:27, NKJV).

The Splits Pose

Associated with Hanuman, a monkey god, this pose signifies devotion and service. Practicing this pose can symbolize a spiritual connection with Hanuman.

- Warning Sign: Engaging in devotional poses to deities invites non-Christian spiritual influences.

- Scripture Warning: "You shall not make for yourselves a carved image—any likeness of anything that is in heaven above, or that is in the earth beneath, or that is in the water under the earth" (Exodus 20:4, NKJV).

The Standing Pose

This pose, representing Tadasana, symbolizes a mountain and stability. It's dedicated to the strength and endurance of deities.

- Warning Sign: Seeking stability and strength through poses dedicated to deities instead of relying on God.

- Scripture Warning: "The Lord is my rock and my fortress and my deliverer; my God, my strength, in whom I will trust" (Psalm 18:2, NKJV).

The Goddess Pose

Dedicated to various female deities, this pose symbolizes feminine power and fertility. Practicing this pose can invite the essence of these deities.

- Warning Sign: Invoking feminine deities contradicts the Christian understanding of God's power and creation.

- Scripture Warning: "For there is one God and one Mediator between God and men, the Man Christ Jesus" (1 Timothy 2:5, NKJV).

Shiva is "The Lord of Yoga"

This chapter highlights Shiva's central role in yoga as the destroyer and transformer. Engaging in yoga practices can subtly align a believer with Shiva's influence.

- Warning Sign: Associating with a deity whose attributes conflict with Christian teachings.

- Scripture Warning: "Therefore put to death your members which are on the earth: fornication, uncleanness, passion, evil desire, and covetousness, which is idolatry" (Colossians 3:5 NKJV).

The Deception and Appeal to Believers

Yoga is designed to invite deities into the practitioner's life. These spiritual practices can subtly deceive born-again believers, leading them away from their faith. Imagine a deity responding to why they are present in a believer's life: "Hey!? I was minding my business and they called me and invited me to be yoked with them. I didn't call them, so that's why they do as I say."

Scripture Warnings:

- "You shall have no other gods before Me" (Exodus 20:3, NKJV).

- "And what agreement does the temple of God have with idols? For you are the temple of the living God" (2 Corinthians 6:16, NKJV).

- "Do not turn to idols, nor make for yourselves molded gods: I am the Lord your God" (Leviticus 19:4, NKJV).

- "Now the Spirit expressly says that in later times some will depart from the faith, giving heed to deceiving spirits and doctrines of demons" (1 Timothy 4:1, NKJV).

Hope for Deliverance

For those who have practiced yoga, there is hope for deliverance. Recognize the spiritual dangers, repent, and seek God's forgiveness. Turn to Him for spiritual cleansing and renewal.

Steps for Deliverance:

1. **Acknowledge and Renounce**: Recognize the spiritual implications and renounce any association with yoga practices.

- Scripture: "And the times of this ignorance God winked at; but now commandeth all men everywhere to repent" (Acts 17:30, NKJV).

2. Repent and Seek Forgiveness: Confess and repent, asking God for forgiveness and cleansing.

- Scripture: "If we confess our sins, He is faithful and just to forgive us our sins and to cleanse us from all unrighteousness" (1 John 1:9, NKJV).

3. Renew Your Mind: Immerse yourself in Scripture to renew your mind and fortify your faith.

- Scripture: "And do not be conformed to this world, but be transformed by the renewing of your mind, that you may prove what is that good and acceptable and perfect will of God" (Romans 12:2, NKJV).

4. Engage in Godly Practices: Replace yoga with Christian practices like prayer, Bible study, and worship.

- Scripture**: "Meditate on these things; give yourself entirely to them, that your progress may be evident to all" (1 Timothy 4:15, NKJV).

5. Seek Fellowship and Accountability: Surround yourself with a supportive Christian community.

- Scripture: "And let us consider one another in order to stir up love and good works, not forsaking the assembling of ourselves together, as is the manner of some, but exhorting one another, and so much the more as you see the Day approaching" (Hebrews 10:24-25, NKJV).

Scripture for Encouragement:

- "Therefore if the Son makes you free, you shall be free indeed" (John 8:36, NKJV).

- "If we confess our sins, He is faithful and just to forgive us our sins and to cleanse us from all unrighteousness" (1 John 1:9, NKJV).

Conclusion

Yoga is not something to be played with; it carries spiritual risks that can lead believers away from God. By recognizing these dangers, repenting, and seeking God's guidance, deliverance is possible. Remain vigilant, fortify your faith, and keep your spiritual focus on God alone.

What God Says About Practicing Yoga

Scriptures Warning Against Worshiping Other Gods, Practicing Yoga, Offering Up to Idols, and Worshiping Demons

1. **Exodus 20:3**: "You shall have no other gods before Me."

2. **Deuteronomy 6:14**: "You shall not go after other gods, the gods of the peoples who are all around you."

3. **Joshua 23:7**: "And lest you go among these nations, these who remain among you. You shall not make mention of the name of their gods, nor cause anyone to swear by them; you shall not serve them nor bow down to them."

4. **2 Kings 17:35**: "With whom the Lord had made a covenant and charged them, saying: 'You shall not fear other gods, nor bow down to them nor serve them nor sacrifice to them.'"

5. **Psalm 81:9**: "There shall be no foreign god among you; nor shall you worship any foreign god."

6. **Isaiah 42:8**: "I am the Lord, that is My name; and My glory I will not give to another, nor My praise to carved images."

7. **Jeremiah 25:6**: "Do not go after other gods to serve them and worship them, and do not provoke Me to anger with the works of your hands; and I will not harm you."

8. **Daniel 3:18**: "But if not, let it be known to you, O king, that we do not serve your gods, nor will we worship the gold image which you have set up."

9. **Hosea 13:4**: "Yet I am the Lord your God ever since the land of Egypt, and you shall know no God but Me; for there is no savior besides Me."

10. **1 Corinthians 10:14**: "Therefore, my beloved, flee from idolatry."

11. **2 Corinthians 6:16**: "And what agreement has the temple of God with idols? For you are the temple of the living God. As God has said: 'I will dwell in them and walk among them. I

will be their God, and they shall be My people.'"

12. **Galatians 5:19-21**: "Now the works of the flesh are evident, which are: adultery, fornication, uncleanness, lewdness, idolatry, sorcery, hatred, contentions, jealousies, outbursts of wrath, selfish ambitions, dissensions, heresies, envy, murders, drunkenness, revelries, and the like; of which I tell you beforehand, just as I also told you in time past, that those who practice such things will not inherit the kingdom of God."

13. **Colossians 3:5**: "Therefore put to death your members which are on the earth: fornication, uncleanness, passion, evil desire, and covetousness, which is idolatry."

14. **1 Peter 4:3**: "For we have spent enough of our past lifetime in doing the will of the Gentiles—when we walked in lewdness, lusts, drunkenness, revelries, drinking parties, and abominable idolatries."

15. **1 John 5:21**: "Little children, keep yourselves from idols. Amen."

16. **Revelation 9:20**: "But the rest of mankind, who were not killed by these plagues, did not repent of the works of their hands, that they should not worship demons, and idols of gold, silver, brass, stone, and wood, which can neither see nor hear nor walk."

17. **Revelation 22:15**: "But outside are dogs and sorcerers and sexually immoral and murderers and idolaters, and whoever loves and practices a lie."

18. **Deuteronomy 12:30**: "Take heed to yourself that you are not ensnared to follow them, after they are destroyed from before you, and that you do not inquire after their gods, saying, 'How did these nations serve their gods? I also will do likewise.'"

19. **Deuteronomy 13:1-3**: "If there arises among you a prophet or a dreamer of dreams, and he gives you a sign or a wonder, and the sign or the wonder comes to pass, of which he spoke to you, saying, 'Let us go after other gods'—which you have not known—'and let us serve them,' you shall not listen to the words of that prophet or that dreamer of dreams, for the Lord your God is testing you to know whether

you love the Lord your God with all your heart and with all your soul."

20. **Judges 10:14**: "Go and cry out to the gods which you have chosen; let them deliver you in your time of distress."

21. **1 Samuel 7:3**: "Then Samuel spoke to all the house of Israel, saying, 'If you return to the Lord with all your hearts, then put away the foreign gods and the Ashtoreths from among you, and prepare your hearts for the Lord, and serve Him only; and He will deliver you from the hand of the Philistines.'"

22. **1 Kings 18:21**: "And Elijah came to all the people, and said, 'How long will you falter between two opinions? If the Lord is God, follow Him; but if Baal, follow him.' But the people answered him not a word."

23. **2 Kings 17:33**: "They feared the Lord, yet served their own gods—according to the rituals of the nations from among whom they were carried away."

24. **2 Chronicles 14:3**: "For he removed the altars of the foreign gods and the high places,

and broke down the sacred pillars and cut down the wooden images."

25. **2 Chronicles 33:15**: "He took away the foreign gods and the idol from the house of the Lord, and all the altars that he had built in the mount of the house of the Lord and in Jerusalem; and he cast them out of the city."

These scriptures serve as a reminder of the importance of staying true to the worship of the one true God and avoiding practices and beliefs that lead to idolatry and the worship of other gods.

Bonus Section

More Poses and What They Mean

Cobra Pose (Bhujangasana)

The Cobra Pose, or Bhujangasana, is dedicated to the serpent deity often associated with Shiva. This pose symbolizes the awakening of spiritual energy within the practitioner, a concept rooted in the rise of Kundalini energy. For Christians, practicing Bhujangasana could lead to the invocation of this serpent energy, which directly contradicts Christian teachings. By engaging in this pose, you might awaken energies and spirits that stand against the Holy Spirit. Consider the spiritual peril: are you inviting demonic forces into your life under the guise of physical exercise? Reflect on the eternal consequences—embracing Bhujangasana may lead to a spiritual awakening that draws you away from Christ's light.

Scripture Warning: "Do not turn to idols or make for yourselves any gods of cast metal: I am the Lord your God." (Leviticus 19:4)

Hope for Deliverance: "Submit yourselves therefore to God. Resist the devil, and he will flee from you." (James 4:7)

Lotus Pose (Padmasana)

The Lotus Pose, or Padmasana, is one of the most iconic yoga poses, symbolizing purity and enlightenment. This pose is often associated with various Hindu deities, including Lakshmi and Brahma, who are depicted sitting in the lotus position. For Christians, sitting in Padmasana can be a subtle act of aligning with these deities, contradicting the First Commandment. The Bible warns against the worship of other gods, and by practicing Padmasana, you may find your meditation and spiritual focus shifting towards Hindu concepts. Reflect deeply on this: are you seeking enlightenment in a manner that could lead to spiritual deception? Embracing the Lotus Pose might open your heart to teachings that steer you away from the truth of the Gospel.

Scripture Warning: "You shall have no other gods before me." (Exodus 20:3)

Hope for Deliverance: "The Lord is near to all who call on him, to all who call on him in truth." (Psalm 145:18)

Fish Pose (Matsyasana)

Matsyasana, or the Fish Pose, is named after Matsya, the fish incarnation of Lord Vishnu. This pose is believed to bring about spiritual awakening and enlightenment. For Christians, aligning with Matsya through this pose poses a risk of spiritual confusion. The Bible emphasizes worshiping God alone, and practicing Matsyasana might draw your heart towards the mythologies of Vishnu's incarnations. Reflect on the consequences: in your pursuit of physical flexibility and spiritual awakening, are you inadvertently opening your soul to the influence of a false god? Embrace this pose, and you may find your spiritual journey diverging from the path laid out by Christ.

Scripture Warning: "Take care that you be not ensnared to follow them, after they have been destroyed before you, and that you do not inquire about their gods, saying, 'How did these nations serve their gods?'—that I also may do the same." (Deuteronomy 12:30)

Hope for Deliverance: "I sought the Lord, and he answered me and delivered me from all my fears." (Psalm 34:4)

Peacock Pose (Mayurasana)

Mayurasana, or the Peacock Pose, symbolizes beauty and the divine vehicle of Lord Krishna. This pose is believed to purify the practitioner's body and soul. For Christians, engaging in Mayurasana can be spiritually perilous. The Bible warns against the worship of other gods, and aligning with Krishna through this pose might lead to spiritual impurities. Reflect on the spiritual risks: are you seeking purification through a practice that could taint your soul with idolatrous influences? Embracing Mayurasana could lead you to admire and invoke qualities that draw you away from the purity and devotion found in Christ alone.

Scripture Warning: "They sacrificed to demons that were no gods, to gods they had never known, to new gods that had come recently, whom your fathers had never dreaded." (Deuteronomy 32:17)

Hope for Deliverance "For he has rescued us from the dominion of darkness and brought us into the kingdom of the Son he loves." (Colossians 1:13)

Eagle Pose (Garudasana)

Garudasana, or the Eagle Pose, honors Garuda, the mythical bird and mount of Lord Vishnu. This pose embodies vigilance, strength, and protection. For Christians, practicing Garudasana could lead to a subtle shift in spiritual allegiance. The Bible cautions against idolatry, and by embodying Garuda's qualities, you might find yourself spiritually soaring towards Vishnu rather than God. Reflect deeply: in your pursuit of physical and spiritual strength, are you inviting the influence of a mythical bird deity? Embrace this pose, and you may find your spiritual protection and strength derived from sources contrary to your faith in Christ.

Scripture Warning: "Do not be unequally yoked with unbelievers. For what partnership has righteousness with lawlessness? Or what fellowship has light with darkness?" (2 Corinthians 6:14)

Hope for Deliverance: "The Lord is my rock and my fortress and my deliverer, my God, my rock, in whom I take refuge, my shield, and the horn of my salvation, my stronghold." (Psalm 18:2)

Bridge Pose (Setu Bandhasana)

Setu Bandhasana, or the Bridge Pose, is often linked to the concept of bridging the earthly and divine realms. It is associated with Lord Rama, who built a bridge to rescue his wife, Sita. For Christians, practicing this pose might symbolically connect you to Hindu narratives. The Bible emphasizes the unique bridge Jesus built between humanity and God. Reflect on the spiritual symbolism: in seeking to bridge your physical and spiritual realms, are you inadvertently aligning with Hindu tales and divinities? Embracing the Bridge Pose could lead you to spiritually connect with a mythology that diverts from the salvific work of Christ.

Scripture Warning: "For there is one God, and there is one mediator between God and men, the man Christ Jesus." (1 Timothy 2:5)

Hope for Deliverance: "Jesus answered, 'I am the way and the truth and the life. No one comes to the Father except through me.'" (John 14:6)

Lion Pose (Simhasana)

Simhasana, or the Lion Pose, is associated with Narasimha, the lion-headed avatar of Vishnu. This pose is believed to bring courage and strength. For Christians, invoking Narasimha through this pose is spiritually hazardous. The Bible strictly forbids worshiping other gods, and by embodying the qualities of Narasimha, you may be inviting his fierce, protective spirit into your life. Reflect on the spiritual dangers: in seeking courage and strength, are you aligning with a deity who stands outside the Christian faith? Embrace this pose, and you might find your spiritual boldness sourced from a lion-headed god rather than the Lion of Judah, Jesus Christ.

Scripture Warning: "You shall not bow down to them or serve them, for I the Lord your God am a jealous God." (Exodus 20:5)

Hope for Deliverance: "The Lord is my light and my salvation; whom shall I fear? The Lord is the stronghold of my life; of whom shall I be afraid?" (Psalm 27:1)

Frog Pose (Bhekasana)

Bhekasana, or the Frog Pose, is linked to the frog, a symbol of fertility and transformation in Hindu mythology, often associated with Varuna, the god of water. For Christians, practicing this pose might symbolically align you with pagan fertility rituals. The Bible warns against participating in practices linked to other deities. Reflect on the spiritual implications: in your pursuit of physical flexibility and transformation, are you opening your soul to influences contrary to the purity of Christ? Embracing Bhekasana could lead to a spiritual metamorphosis that diverges from the transformation offered through Jesus.

Scripture Warning: "Therefore, my beloved, flee from idolatry." (1 Corinthians 10:14)

Hope for Deliverance: "For I know the plans I have for you, declares the Lord, plans for welfare and not for evil, to give you a future and a hope." (Jeremiah 29:11)Dancer Pose (Natarajasana)

Natarajasana, or the Dancer Pose, honors Nataraja, the dancing form of Lord Shiva. This pose symbolizes cosmic dance and divine energy. For Christians, practicing Natarajasana is spiritually perilous. The Bible strictly admonishes against aligning with other gods, and Shiva's cosmic dance represents a cycle of creation and destruction outside Christian teachings. Reflect deeply: in your pursuit of physical grace and spiritual energy, are you invoking the cosmic dance of a Hindu deity? Embrace this pose, and you might find your spiritual rhythm aligned with Shiva's dance rather than the eternal life found in Christ.

Scripture Warning: "Take no part in the unfruitful works of darkness, but instead expose them." (Ephesians 5:11)

Hope for Deliverance: "For God gave us a spirit not of fear but of power and love and self-control." (2 Timothy 1:7)

Hero Pose (Virasana)

Virasana, or the Hero Pose, is associated with various warrior deities in Hindu mythology, symbolizing courage and inner strength. For Christians, practicing Virasana could lead to spiritual confusion. The Bible emphasizes finding strength and courage in God alone, and by embodying the qualities of Hindu warrior deities, you might find your spiritual heroism misplaced.

Reflect on the spiritual risks: in seeking to embody heroism and strength, are you drawing from a source outside the Christian faith? Embrace Virasana, and you may find your spiritual valor aligned with mythological heroes rather than the true heroism exemplified by Christ.

Scripture Warning: "Be strong and courageous. Do not fear or be in dread of them, for it is the Lord your God who goes with you. He will not leave you or forsake you." (Deuteronomy 31:6)

Hope for Deliverance: "The Lord is my strength and my shield; in him my heart trusts, and I am helped; my heart exults, and with my song I give thanks to him." (Psalm 28:7)

Downward Dog Pose (Adho Mukha Svanasana)

Adho Mukha Svanasana, or the Downward Dog Pose, is often linked to the deity Hanuman, the monkey god, symbolizing devotion and strength. For Christians, practicing this pose can be spiritually risky. The Bible warns against idol worship, and aligning with Hanuman through this pose might lead to spiritual confusion. Reflect on the consequences: in seeking physical flexibility and strength, are you inadvertently drawing your devotion away from God and towards a Hindu deity? Embracing the Downward Dog Pose could lead to a spiritual allegiance that conflicts with your faith in Christ.

Scripture Warning: "You shall not make for yourselves a carved image, or any likeness of anything that is in heaven above, or that is on the earth beneath, or that is in the water under the earth. You shall not bow down to them or serve them, for I the Lord your God am a jealous God." (Exodus 20:4-5)

Hope for Deliverance: "But the Lord is faithful. He will establish you and guard you against the evil one." (2 Thessalonians 3:3)

Headstand (Sirsasana)

Sirsasana, or the Headstand, is often referred to as the king of yoga poses and is associated with the inversion of worldly perspectives, a concept deeply rooted in Hindu spirituality. This pose can symbolize seeing the world through a different lens, often aligned with the god Shiva. For Christians, this inversion can lead to a spiritual perspective that conflicts with the teachings of the Bible. Reflect on the spiritual risks: are you seeking enlightenment through a practice that inverts your spiritual focus away from Christ? Embracing Sirsasana could lead to a perspective that aligns more with Hindu philosophy than with Christian truth.

Scripture Warning: "Woe to those who call evil good and good evil, who put darkness for light and light for darkness, who put bitter for sweet and sweet for bitter!" (Isaiah 5:20)

Hope for Deliverance: "Do not be conformed to this world, but be transformed by the renewal of your mind, that by testing you may discern what is the will of God, what is good and acceptable and perfect." (Romans 12:2)

Child's Pose (Balasana)

Balasana, or the Child's Pose, is associated with a return to innocence and surrender, often linked to the deity Krishna as a divine child. For Christians, practicing this pose might symbolize a surrender to a deity outside the Christian faith. The Bible emphasizes surrendering to God alone, and by adopting Balasana, you might find your spiritual surrender misplaced. Reflect on the implications: in seeking peace and innocence, are you inadvertently surrendering to a concept that diverts from the Christian faith? Embracing the Child's Pose could lead you to a spiritual state that aligns with Krishna rather than Christ.

Scripture Warning: "You shall have no other gods before me." (Exodus 20:3)

Hope for Deliverance: "Come to me, all who labor and are heavy laden, and I will give you rest." (Matthew 11:28)

The Deception and Appeal to Believers

Yoga is designed to invite deities into the practitioner's life. These spiritual practices can subtly deceive born-again believers, leading them away from their faith. Imagine a deity responding to why they are present in a believer's life: "Hey!? I was minding my business and they called me and invited me to be yoked with them. I didn't call them, so that's why they do as I say."

Scripture Warnings:

- "You shall have no other gods before Me" (Exodus 20:3, NKJV).
- "And what agreement has the temple of God with idols? For you are the temple of the living God" (2 Corinthians 6:16, NKJV).
- "Do not turn to idols, nor make for yourselves molded gods: I am the Lord your God" (Leviticus 19:4, NKJV).
- "Now the Spirit expressly says that in latter times some will depart from the faith, giving heed to deceiving spirits and doctrines of demons" (1 Timothy 4:1, NKJV).

Hope for Deliverance

For those who have practiced yoga, there is hope for deliverance. Recognize the spiritual dangers, repent, and seek God's forgiveness. Turn to Him for spiritual cleansing and renewal.

Steps for Deliverance:

1. Acknowledge and Renounce: Recognize the spiritual implications and renounce any association with yoga practices.

- Scripture: "And the times of this ignorance God winked at; but now commandeth all men everywhere to repent" (Acts 17:30, NKJV).

2. Repent and Seek Forgiveness: Confess and repent, asking God for forgiveness and cleansing.

- Scripture: "If we confess our sins, He is faithful and just to forgive us our sins and to cleanse us from all unrighteousness" (1 John 1:9, NKJV).

3. Renew Your Mind: Immerse yourself in Scripture to renew your mind and fortify your faith.

- Scripture: "And do not be conformed to this world, but be transformed by the renewing of your mind, that you may prove what is that good and acceptable and perfect will of God" (Romans 12:2, NKJV).

4. Engage in Godly Practices: Replace yoga with Christian practices like prayer, Bible study, and worship.

- Scripture: "Meditate on these things; give yourself entirely to them, that your progress may be evident to all" (1 Timothy 4:15, NKJV).

5. Seek Fellowship and Accountability: Surround yourself with a supportive Christian community.

- Scripture: "And let us consider one another in order to stir up love and good works, not forsaking the assembling of ourselves together, as is the manner of some, but exhorting one another, and so much the more as you see the Day approaching" (Hebrews 10:24-25, NKJV).

Scripture for Encouragement:

- "Therefore if the Son makes you free, you shall be free indeed" (John 8:36, NKJV).
- "If we confess our sins, He is faithful and just to forgive us our sins and to cleanse us from all unrighteousness" (1 John 1:9, NKJV).

Conclusion

In concluding this exploration of the spiritual dangers of yoga for Christians, it's important to clarify that there is nothing inherently wrong with exercising for health. Physical fitness is beneficial, and caring for our bodies is a good practice. However, the issue arises when these exercises are connected to the three dimensions of worship, unknowingly inviting spirits into one's life. This hidden spiritual aspect can lead to profound negative consequences for believers.

Throughout this book, we've examined how various yoga poses, often perceived as mere physical exercises, actually serve as acts of worship to Hindu deities. Let's revisit each chapter and its warnings, emphasizing the potential spiritual pitfalls.

We began with the **Tree Pose**, which, while appearing harmless, symbolizes alignment with nature and Hindu deities. This pose subtly opens the door to spiritual influences contrary to biblical teachings. It serves as a reminder that our strength and stability should come from God alone.

Next, we explored the **Warrior I, II, and III Poses**. These poses celebrate the strength and power of a warrior deity. As Christians, we are called to rely on God's strength, not our own or that of any spiritual being. Engaging in these poses can lead believers to unintentionally honor deities rather than God.

The **Half Moon Pose** symbolizes balance and serenity through the embodiment of a moon god. However, true peace comes from God alone, not from imitating or invoking the essence of a deity. This chapter highlighted the subtle deception present in seemingly peaceful practices.

We discussed the **Splits Pose**, associated with the deity Hanuman. This pose, often viewed as a testament to flexibility, actually represents devotion and surrender to a god. Such practices can blur the lines of faith, leading believers away from their devotion to Christ.

The **Standing Pose**, though promoting physical stability, symbolizes reliance on oneself or deities rather than on God. As Christians, we are reminded that the Lord is our rock and fortress, and our stability should rest solely on Him.

The **Goddess Pose** invites practitioners to channel feminine energy, often associated with specific goddesses. While it might seem empowering, it involves invoking the essence of deities, leading believers away from the true source of strength—God. This chapter emphasized the dangers of blending spiritual beliefs and practices.

The chapter on **Shiva as "The Lord of Yoga"** delved into the significance of Shiva in yoga philosophy. Understanding that Shiva is revered as the ultimate yogi reveals the deep spiritual roots of yoga, contrasting with the Christian belief in the one true God. Participating in practices that honor Shiva can lead to spiritual confusion and conflict.

In discussing **The Ultimate Goal of Yoga** We explored how the practice aims for spiritual awakening and union with the divine, which is fundamentally different from Christian beliefs about salvation and relationship with God. The ultimate goal of yoga, becoming one with these deities, is a stark warning for believers. It's a reminder that the spiritual world is real, and connecting with it through yoga can have serious consequences.

Finally, in **My Appeal to You** We urged believers to recognize the spiritual dimensions of yoga and the potential dangers it poses to their faith. Engaging in practices that invite spiritual entities into one's life can lead to bondage, deception, and a gradual drift away from God.

Stories of Deliverance

Consider the story of Sarah, a devoted Christian who began practicing yoga purely for its physical benefits. She appreciated the flexibility and calm it brought her. Over time, however, she noticed subtle changes in her spiritual life. She began experiencing anxiety and a sense of emptiness, despite regular church attendance and prayer. Unbeknownst to her, the yoga practices she considered harmless were opening her up to spiritual influences.

One day, after a yoga session focused on a particular pose, Sarah had a vivid dream. In it, she felt a dark presence and heard a voice saying, "You called me." Confused and frightened, she sought counsel from a trusted Christian mentor who prayed with her, guiding her to renounce any spiritual ties formed through yoga. Sarah realized that what she thought was just exercise had deeper spiritual implications. She repented and sought deliverance through prayer and the Word of God. Verses like Ephesians 6:12, which states, "For we do not wrestle against flesh and blood, but against principalities, against powers, against the rulers of the darkness of this age," resonated deeply with her.

Her journey of deliverance was challenging, but she found freedom and peace through Christ. She replaced her yoga practice with other forms of exercise that honored God and strengthened her faith. Sarah's story serves as a powerful reminder that while yoga might seem harmless, its spiritual roots can have profound negative effects on a believer's life.

Rachel's Awakening to Spiritual Warfare

Rachel was a devoted Christian and yoga enthusiast who began practicing yoga as a way to alleviate stress and improve her physical health. She enjoyed the physical benefits and the sense of relaxation yoga provided after a long day at work. Over time, Rachel started attending more advanced yoga classes, including ones that incorporated meditation and chanting.

As Rachel delved deeper into her yoga practice, she began experiencing unsettling occurrences and a sense of spiritual unease. She started having vivid dreams of strange symbols and encounters with shadowy figures, which left her feeling spiritually drained and fearful. Concerned about these experiences, Rachel sought counsel from her pastor.

Through prayer and biblical guidance, Rachel came to realize that the spiritual elements within yoga were conflicting with her Christian faith. She learned about the concept of spiritual warfare and how engaging in practices that invoke spiritual entities can open doors to negative spiritual influences. With the support of her church community, Rachel made the decision to step away from yoga and instead focused on prayer, worship, and studying Scripture.

As Rachel distanced herself from yoga, she experienced a gradual sense of spiritual renewal and clarity. The unsettling dreams ceased, and she felt a renewed connection with God. Rachel's journey taught her the importance of spiritual discernment and staying rooted in biblical truth. She now shares her story to educate others about the spiritual dangers of practices that conflict with Christian beliefs, encouraging them to seek God's guidance in all aspects of their lives.

Jason's Struggle with Spiritual Oppression

Jason was a young Christian man who turned to yoga to improve his flexibility and physical fitness. Initially, he viewed yoga as a harmless exercise and relaxation technique. However, as Jason continued his yoga practice, he noticed subtle changes in his spiritual life.

He began to feel spiritually distant from God and experienced a sense of heaviness and oppression in his spirit. Jason also started having disturbing thoughts and dreams that left him feeling anxious and unsettled. Unsure of the cause, Jason sought advice from his mentor at church.

Through prayer and spiritual discernment, Jason realized that his involvement in yoga had inadvertently opened doors to spiritual influences that were contrary to his Christian beliefs. He learned about the importance of guarding his heart and mind against practices that could lead him away from God. With support from his family and church community, Jason made the decision to stop practicing yoga and instead focused on strengthening his relationship with God through prayer, worship, and fellowship.

As Jason turned his focus back to his faith, he experienced a gradual sense of spiritual healing and restoration. The feelings of oppression lifted, and he regained a deep sense of peace and joy in his relationship with God. Jason now shares his story to warn others about the spiritual dangers of engaging in yoga practices that conflict with biblical teachings, encouraging them to seek spiritual discernment in God's truth.

Maria's Journey to Spiritual Clarity

Maria was a middle-aged woman who started practicing yoga as a way to manage stress and improve her overall well-being. She found solace in the calming effects of yoga and enjoyed the sense of community she found in her yoga classes. However, as Maria deepened her involvement in yoga, she began to experience unsettling spiritual encounters.

She started having vivid dreams of unfamiliar people that felt evil and felt a growing sense of spiritual confusion. Maria also noticed changes in her emotional state, experiencing bouts of anxiety and fear. Concerned about these experiences, Maria sought guidance from her pastor and a Christian counselor.

Through prayer and biblical counseling, Maria gained clarity on the spiritual implications of her yoga practice. She learned about the dangers of spiritual syncretism and how engaging in practices that invoke spiritual entities can lead to spiritual bondage. With support from her church community, Maria made the decision to step away from yoga and focus on cultivating her relationship with God through prayer, worship, and studying Scripture.

As Maria committed herself to spiritual growth and discernment, she experienced a profound sense of peace and spiritual clarity. The unsettling dreams and feelings of confusion gradually subsided, and Maria felt a renewed sense of purpose in her faith journey. Maria now shares her story to educate others about the importance of spiritual discernment and staying true to biblical teachings, encouraging them to seek God's wisdom in every decision they make.

Daniel's Battle with Spiritual Deception

Daniel was a young man who grew up in a Christian family and had a passion for physical fitness. He started practicing yoga to improve his flexibility and enhance his athletic performance. At first, Daniel viewed yoga as a purely physical exercise and relaxation technique.

However, as Daniel continued his yoga practice, he began to experience spiritual challenges. He noticed a shift in his thoughts and emotions, feeling increasingly detached from his Christian beliefs. Daniel also started having recurring dreams of encountering spiritual beings and felt a sense of spiritual oppression.

Troubled by these experiences, Daniel sought counsel from his pastor and a Christian mentor. Through prayer and spiritual guidance, Daniel came to understand that his involvement in yoga had inadvertently opened doors to spiritual deception and influence. He learned about the importance of spiritual discernment and staying rooted in God's truth.

With the support of his church community, Daniel made the difficult decision to stop practicing yoga and instead focused on prayer, worship, and biblical meditation. As Daniel turned his focus back to his faith, he experienced a gradual sense of spiritual liberation and renewal.

The troubling dreams and feelings of spiritual oppression gradually diminished, and Daniel felt a renewed sense of peace and clarity in his relationship with God.

Daniel now shares his story to warn others about the spiritual dangers of practices that conflict with Christian beliefs, encouraging them to prioritize their relationship with God and seek His wisdom in all aspects of their lives.

Mary's Discovery of Spiritual Truth

Mary was a young woman who was drawn to yoga as a way to find inner peace and spiritual enlightenment. She immersed herself in various yoga practices, including meditation and chanting, believing they would help her achieve spiritual growth and fulfillment.

As Mary deepened her involvement in yoga, she began to experience unsettling spiritual manifestations. She started having vivid dreams and visions of encountering spiritual entities and felt a growing sense of spiritual confusion.Mary also noticed changes in her emotional well-being, experiencing mood swings and bouts of anxiety.

Disturbed by these experiences, Mary sought guidance from her Christian friends and a trusted spiritual advisor. Through prayer and biblical counseling, Mary gained clarity on the spiritual implications of her yoga practice. She learned about the dangers of spiritual syncretism and the importance of guarding her heart and mind against practices that could lead her away from God.

With the support of her church community, Mary made the decision to step away from yoga and instead focused on deepening her relationship with God through prayer, worship, and studying Scripture. As Mary surrendered her life to God's guidance and truth, she experienced a profound sense of spiritual liberation and healing.

The troubling dreams and spiritual manifestations gradually subsided, and Mary felt a renewed sense of purpose and clarity in her faith journey. Mary now shares her story to educate others about the spiritual dangers of practices that conflict with Christian beliefs, encouraging them to seek God's wisdom and discernment in all aspects of their lives.

These stories illustrate the varied experiences of individuals who found themselves entangled in yoga practices that conflicted with their Christian faith. Through prayer, guidance, and the support of their church communities, each person experienced deliverance and spiritual renewal. Their journeys highlight the importance of spiritual discernment, prayerful reflection, and seeking God's truth in navigating spiritual challenges. May their stories inspire and encourage others to prioritize their relationship with God and seek His wisdom in all aspects of their lives.

Closing Thoughts

As Christians, we must be vigilant and discerning about the practices we engage in. While exercise is essential for our physical health, we must ensure that our activities do not compromise our spiritual well-being. Connecting with the three dimensions of worship in yoga—devotion, mantra, and spiritual unity—can lead us down a path we never intended to tread.

This book serves as a warning to Christians about the dangers of practicing yoga. Each chapter has highlighted how seemingly innocuous poses and practices can have deep spiritual implications. The goal of yoga is not just physical health but a spiritual journey that may conflict with our faith.

Remember, our bodies are temples of the Holy Spirit (1 Corinthians 6:19). We are called to glorify God in all that we do. As you consider your exercise choices, prioritize your spiritual health and seek activities that align with your faith in Christ.

If you find yourself entangled in yoga or other practices that lead you away from God, know that there is hope for deliverance. Turn to God, seek His forgiveness, and find strength in His Word. Surround yourself with fellow believers who can support you in your spiritual journey.

Let Sarah's story be an encouragement to you. She found freedom and renewed faith through Christ, and so can you. Embrace exercises that honor God and strengthen your relationship with Him, ensuring that your spiritual journey leads you closer to the one true God, not away from Him.

May God bless you and guide you in all your endeavors, keeping you firmly rooted in His love and truth.

About The Author

Meet Dr. Anthony Ladson, a passionate theologian and entrepreneur dedicated to making a difference. Since earning his Doctorate in Theology with a minor in Eschatology in 2006, he has been on a mission to inspire and uplift others.

As a dynamic speaker, trainer, and coach, Dr. Ladson believes that true growth starts in the mind. His approach has empowered countless individuals to reach their full potential. Balancing his many roles, he successfully manages multiple businesses, showcasing his versatility and unwavering commitment to excellence.

Dr. Ladson cherishes his family life with his loving wife, Kim, and their daughter, Jessica. His ultimate goal is to transform a billion lives through the power of the Word of God.

Explore his latest books and teachings, and take advantage of the free resources he offers to support your journey of personal and spiritual growth.

For more information or bookings, feel free to reach out and connect with Dr. Anthony Ladson

The Mysteries of The Bible

Free Download

I'm Born Again Now What ? E-Book

bit.ly/3UUh0uQ

Latest Release

Master Key To The Kingdom Book

bit.ly/3P4O92V

Click Here To Subscribe My Youtube Channel

www.ingramcontent.com/pod-product-compliance
Lightning Source LLC
Chambersburg PA
CBHW052101230426
43662CB00036B/1750